The Dangerous Country of Love and Marriage

The Dangerous Country of Love and Marriage

Amy Leigh Wicks

AUCKLAND
UNIVERSITY
PRESS

First published 2019
Auckland University Press
University of Auckland
Private Bag 92019
Auckland 1142
New Zealand
www.press.auckland.ac.nz

ISBN 978 1 86940 897 8

Published with the assistance of Creative New Zealand

ARTS COUNCIL OF NEW ZEALAND TOI AOTEAROA

A catalogue record for this book is available from the National Library of New Zealand

Book design by Katrina Duncan
Cover design by Scott Crickett

Cover design credits: NZTopo50-BQ31 by Land Information New Zealand is licensed
under CC BY 4.0, recoloured from original; '1899 map of Manhattan showing streetcar lines'
from Wikimedia Commons is licensed under Public Domain, cropped and recoloured from original.

Printed by Everbest Printing Investment Ltd, China

For Matthew,
with love

CONTENTS

CREATION STORY

I was alone in the womb
breathing the water of God
through my little gills.

I came shivering—gasping
to the light—my mother
's face a smear of pink.

To be held against a wall
with her heart on the other side—
this was my first sadness.

I loved the taste
of all my Play-Doh—red
was my favourite. Father

fed me pink grapefruit hearts
on a tiny silver spoon—I tore
each chamber apart with my teeth.

TEND

Get the ones that grow up between the cracks
my mother says, leaning over the lemon balm.

She is a sweating, garden-gloved goddess with strong arms
and I am pulling puny weeds from patio squares

thinking about cloud shapes, and the way that boy
touched my back when he walked past me yesterday.

There are peppers, tomatoes, eggplants heavy on the vine
but I don't see them. I see dandelions and cement

and I have barely finished two squares when Mom sends me
to make sandwiches. Things are growing but I don't see them

until fifteen years later in Island Bay. It took the furthest place
from home for me to put on muck boots and feed somebody else's

chickens in earnest. Now I place the tentacled roots of coriander and spring
onions in a jar like they are holy, with a little water, facing the sun.

PSALM I

You know my father's name
is John—impossible. Look at
your little sea with whales
smaller than ice cubes!

The sun was cold
before you touched it,
and now it rages love.

Why make almost
gods of girls like me
who hook the fish
and stomp the grass
and eat popcorn
with glistening fingers
in the centre row of the theatre?

SALT AND LIGHT

The first time he stopped by
the house we were tall
as his belt buckle.

I ride toward the Brooklyn Bridge
from Harlem before sunrise.

I want to be clean
so I need to be cold.
When my lungs scream
and sweat stings my eyes,
it is almost over.

There was no coast to run to
so how could we wash?

Cold black morning
then grey
until the sun blisters
the silver buildings

and I am cold, surrounded by water
and metal.

His stomach is a barrel.
We are too small to see his face.
His breathing is rats
chasing a can in an alley.

Every one that falls (an apple
in his yard) is devoured.

I want to be clean
so I need to be cold.
When my lungs scream
and sweat stings my eyes,
it is almost over.

I am clean and full of salt now.
I am an ocean.

LOG NO. 1

There is no blanket of fog. I am not running through the woods
today. Last night I was swimming and could hear bullets in
the water around me. They sound like *zhzh*, a pleasant sound.
The night before I could feel a man behind me before I saw the
shadow of his hat. He grabbed my arm and I ran and threw myself
down in some shrubs. I could hear a truck or a van racing toward
me. I woke up safe, but barely. I used to have to watch people die
in my dreams. I could hear, smell, feel their blood warm on my
shoulders. Bev from high school said that was nothing. Her sister
used to attend her own funeral in her dreams, night after night for
a whole year. That was after her parents divorced and her stepdad
moved in. He was a taxidermist. She showed me the basement of
hooks and stretched skins of deer and coyote. We weren't supposed
to be down there, drinking her mom's Kahlúa in our milk.

LORETTA

Who doesn't hope
for a fishing net
to come heavy
from the water with
an old locked box
caught in the net?

You might ask
how did the box
swim into the net?
And I might say

that is between
the box and the net.

Some other secrets
come up from the deep.

I have had to open
the door—to let out dust
of another century.
It floated toward
our boat in a sealed urn,
and when I brought it inside
opened it like a genie's bottle.

I mean, Great Grandma danced
for money and the music
still plays after dusk.

I am the woman who dances
for free. Lets the piano rattle
even after the sun
shines through all the windows.

And when I open the door
again it's for air, into another
country. I can feel her smile

where trees are pink
and the lavender sky smells
of salt and sea and the box
on my stoop is still dripping.

DESCENT

Inside the house where I grew up, black mould
spotted the walls. It was years before we knew
it was inside us like lichen on rocks.

On a starry night, do I choose the fruit that's ripe
or wait alone, for one other human, burning
like a roman candle in the dark? There he is,

hands on the other side of the glass, waiting.
There is the question of table or bar, forever
or an hour of open doors all leading to the same room.

If I was a real woman walking toward him across the floor—
but the oysters are cold, dead in their shells, us not speaking.
Here I am, floating above the earth as it yawns, limp roots crinkling the air—

Mother's friend Jill is packing my doll house
telling Mom what an asshole Dad is (they have never met)
asking, aren't I happy she's free? There I am without a mouth screaming
or in bed beside a stranger, waiting for another storm to break.
Great Grandma's china teacups, one fight at a time,
were dropped onto kitchen tiles.

Now the gallery is well lit, my collarbone on display—
I can see the shine of something, waiting in the dark
and I can't say if I will run toward it or away.

REMNANT

Once I said, I want
to be a lawyer, a doctor,
and a ballerina—

I woke twenty years later
writing these poems.

BILDUNGSROMAN

I chose the blue marble with cream in the centre.
I ate the birthday cake but I did not like it.

The cave was not just dark, it was wet
and I slid through tight passes like a snake.

What light flickers through my dreams
to lead me from one question to another?

I have forgiven the things in you I hated most,
which is to say I have forgiven myself. I know

what it cost to buy that string of pearls. It was full
of hope and mistaken. It took me a long time

but I've found what I am looking for and it is not
marriage starting over. Here we are, standing

on either side of the lawn, iron horseshoes in hand,
tossing toward different stakes, almost reaching.

RAPHA

The heavy knots of rope and clinking chains
on rusted pulleys; the dock at dusk unwrites
my plans and sketches a map of the sea
on the back of my eyes.

There I am, pushing a child in a white pram through
rose gardens. There I am pinching sugar snap peas
from the vine, letting them fall into the basket.

I want to be a sailor—no
I want to be lost in the boat
rescued by a sailor and then
shipwrecked on an island with him.

There is the bunting-dressed hotel lobby
where guests shuffle from mini crab cakes to
éclairs, dull from nice champagne, dabbing eyes
as they dance and grow old and confetti the air
with sadness.

Here I am at the edge of a white page large
as a living room, trying to write with a pen
twice my size. There is a giant hand resting
above my head, waiting for me to let go of the pen.

I want it to go like this—no
I want to be surprised by the ending
but completely in control of how it happens.
The pen flies across the page without me.

What is it about the clairvoyant's dirty fingers
grabbing my wrist after breakfast
that does not surprise me? We walk
toward each other through golden air
but we bow to different futures.

There I am, curled up like a child crying out
all of my fears. Here I am, wiping my eyes
to read each word as it is written.

REDOLENT

A shock of dust settles like
tiny geese on the cover of my book

and I remember beginning—a dark
home without walls, in water. Then

Mother opens the china cabinet, reaches
for the cup with faded pink roses.

Two sugars, more milk than tea,
my hands are so tiny, her hands are God's.

Then I am at a payphone when the train stops
near Pisa, fingernails scratching through the soft

of my palms and then the fear is gone and the night
is breathing on me warm, as if I'm in the mouth of a dog.

Then I am home, it was just a tremor and everything
resettles, alive, dead, alive again.

EPIPHANY

I landed drunk in London, fell asleep waiting
for my 11 a.m. train to Newcastle—
God is not above using station attendants
to wake his baby up. I got to her
in a cold rain still clutching my passport,

so happy I cried.
We left for Northumberland before dawn—
extra layers for rain; red lipstick
on my twenty-two-year-old mouth.

I don't know why she took me
to sit at the edge of the cliff
where water breaks rock into salt.

Down the coast three dogs wrestled
in the white surf and were gone,
and it was just us sitting on our
hands for warmth, and then she was gone and

it was just me, alone with the bruise
of a bad decade, finally asking toward the sky
for a little help, shuddering ugly tears until
I was dry in the silence of an answer I'm still
learning to understand.

CANTICLE I

His warm mouth in the snow
better than the first bottle of pinot noir
I finished on the fire escape after Paris.

His coat smells like diesel and pine and soap.
When he walks in the bar I feel the other girls flame.

Come pick me up.

Take me to your castle
to your tent
to your truck.

I'm light-headed but I won't forget.
I'm messy, but I've been told
my eyes are beautiful,
I've got honey under my tongue.
Of course you won't.

I was supposed to be untangled by now.
Tell me where you'll be anyway.
You wouldn't want me
mixing you up with somebody else.

He tells me to wait
and the lights
finally dim before the movie.

One wild mare let loose
and all the chariots forget the war.
It's a black and white, I don't know
who's starring.

Your skin, my God,
your skin, his thumb traces my jaw.

He sits at the old wooden table under a gas lamp,
and blood taps out a rhythm in my throat.

The only way I can think to slow
my breathing is to picture him asleep
in my arms, night after night after night.

UNMAKING

For Félix González-Torres

What began in the womb continues on the porch
twenty-five years later. Did I make myself

the way I am? Staring at the sun until I see
black spots. The line where sky meets sea

could be a seam, hiding a zipper, and then what?
Sure I get down on my knees sometimes.

Everybody's gotta serve someone, and some
days it's too hard to stand. Some prayers

sound a little like echoes. Some modern art looks
a little like my heart, a pile of hard candy

disappearing one colored drop at a time. Who said love
was bad? There is still the problem of skin, but

on the other side of sky and sea is a pile—
every sweet little thing that's been lost.

THE HISTORY OF NEW YORK

The first time I took the train north to see him
it was bitter cold, even the snow was frozen solid.
Does that mean the snow was ice? Does ice sparkle
like shingles on a tarred roof under the moon? I was
cold on the train the whole five hours thinking
about the next fifty years of my life, wondering what I'd make
for the dinner at my neighbour's next week. Maybe I'd find
mini gherkins, spicy wholegrain mustard, pork, ham,
Swiss, and a loaf of Cuban bread, press it all on the grill
like Myrna used to do for staff meals on holiday shifts instead
of paying us time-and-a-half for waiting tables on Christmas Day.

I spent Christmas at St Vincent's where I was born, trying to tell
if the doctors were lying about Grandpa to make it hurt less,
or if they knew what was wrong with him at all.
Dr Solomon came still wearing his yarmulke, pulling green
scrubs on over a red holiday sweater and I felt safe
under the fluorescent lights because he was whistling
and had a walk that said I'm the guy that they call
when they don't know who to call. He told my Catholic family
Larry has gone septic and he's sorry to say he doesn't know
if he'll make it, but he is going in to do surgery now and we
will know soon enough. My parents stayed married
for three months after that conversation, they sat beside
each other watching *Home Alone* on the screen above
my head. Two hours later, Larry, who hadn't had a drop
of water in three days, was drinking Fanta from a straw,
asking for a comb to pull through his thick white hair.

Four days later I was cold on that train riding north thinking
about two days earlier when the man I was going to see
came to see me and touched my wrist and bought me
a strawberry milkshake even though it was snowing out,
because we'd already had a coffee—well, I'd had a coffee
and he had a hot chocolate, but it was still early
and we were mostly strangers drawn to a diner in town
with red vinyl booths and a sign in the window that said open.

PAYSAGE MORALISÉ

After W. H. Auden

He grows up in the valley,
visiting his grandfather's farm, mountains
covered with pines, pines covered with snow. The water
is always cold in the north country. On the south shore of Staten Island
I grow up on fresh mozzarella and Pop-Pop's tomatoes, visit the city
on the ferry. Gran says the man beside us is drinking sorrow

from his paper bag. At eleven I learn to wind my hips, drink sorrel
with snapper and bammy. At twelve it's Chivas Regal with Valle
on his stoop. My throat burns and I'm warm. Valle says Hudson is his city.
Across the river, on the ridgeline of the Catskill Mountains
Rip sleeps on his side. He doesn't wake when I land
in a snow storm at twenty. The river is hunks of frozen water

moving toward Manhattan alongside the train. Water
is everywhere in Venice, holding countless boats just so. Row
after row of cured prosciutto, Chianti, ciabatta, I wander the aisles and
streets. I get lost and it hurts. At twenty-one he leaves the valley
for canyons and rattlesnakes, mountain
passes and rowdy bars. I leave Venice for other old cities,

bruised, eyes down. When I get back to my city
I am silent for a year. I climb down into familiar water
next summer, leaving my tiny mountain
of clothes on barnacled rocks. Can you call washing sorrow
if there are no tears? I am north of Manhattan Valley
by forty blocks, a mermaid, floating between this island

and New Jersey. In my laundromat on 139th, the stainless steel island
piled with bed sheets listens to me finally open up. The city
wanders through me and knows me. He drives south from Casper to Vail
then east. When he finds me, he takes me to the water
and we watch waves break all night. I don't know his sorrow
or his happiness. I want to touch him. The mountains

out west are pink and gold in the morning. No mountains
are here. Manhattan, Staten, my beautiful dirty islands
are not his. He does not know my sorrow
or my happiness but he knows how to hold me. Jersey City
is lit up across the water
almost beautiful. I might be unravelling.

We are floating on the water
when the sun comes up slowly, heavily—
we are drifting further and further from dry land.

LANDING

I married the man on a motorcycle from out west
and left my city, my state, my country for love.
I did not look back. I thought I might turn to salt.

I gave away all my books and received a jar of coffee.
When it rains the grass does not bruise. What came
of saying yes to love? Loneliness, a shock of cold air—

I changed my name but kept rose my favourite tea.
I watched the ocean grow dirt and grass and trees
and I did not remember my name when we landed.

Memory must be spilled to be full again
and I am as much a tulip as a cup, overflowing even
without my things. One kind word can build a kingdom.

Some say love cannot tell light from dark.
I say it does. It works in sand around a melting clock.

MIHIMIHI

Ko SS *Teutonic* tōku waka

My family's canoe was more of a ship,
something like the SS *Teutonic*.

Ko Catskill tōku maunga

The Catskill mountains are mine,
or have been for longer than any other mountains.

Ko Hudson tōku awa

Which river is mine? The Hudson,
that thread of water that pulled my love to me
and me to him, until we tied the knot.

Ko Te Herenga Waka tōku marae

Te Herenga Waka will be my marae.

Nō New York City ahau

I am from New York, I am from far away
across the seas, a little other island.

Ko Matthew John tōku hoa rangatira

Ko John raūa ko Patricia ōku mātua

My parents are John and Patricia,
I feel their names do not tell enough.

Ko Jonathan rāua ko Jason ōku tungāne

I have two older brothers, they are
Jonathan and Jason

Ko Lyndsay tōku teina

and Lyndsay is my little sister.

He tauira tuhituhi ahau

I am a student of writing, of poetry.
What is the Māori word for poetry?

Ko Amy Leigh tōku ingoa

Amy Leigh is my name.

FIRST NIGHT IN AOTEAROA

I am sitting at a stone table
there is a fire behind me
and a candle before me and
it is raining all around and the papers
on the table are soaking wet
with black ink bleeding through.

Two women I do not know
and one whose face I can not
see clearly, keep trying to tell me
a story, but I can not hear
or will not listen. I am staring

intently at the wet paper, smearing the ink
with my fingers and as I do,
faces appear and then turn
into other things, and I can feel
rain on my face and down my
back. The face of my grandmother

becomes a horse and then the horse
turns into me and then I become
a Grecian urn, but before I can see what
will happen to the urn, one of the women
grabs my wrist and I wake, and it is dark,
and what do you think it means?

PSALM II

Why did my purple teeth
sing your hymns more
sweetly than this sober
tongue? I have left New York,
put out every cigarette.
My bed is made each morning
in a quiet room above the sea,
I drink tea afternoon and evening.
Where is the rage of my youth?
My body is young and strong,
limb to limb there is no
imperfection or lack of beauty
and all of its slopes and planes
are boring. I grate ginger root
into a sizzling pan of spring onions
and rare steak. I steam a perfect
bowl of rice, and when I am
full, I am hungry for the edge
of a cliff or the bottom of the deep.
And when I reach that crag
or descend until my fists are full
of black sand, the disappointment
is as dull as the hunger.

SABBATH

He picks the meat off the bones and separates
dark from white meat on the blue speckled plate

while I shred a pile of cabbage
into the silver bowl with carrots for coleslaw.

The rolls are warming in the oven,
cheese sliced onto the small flowered plate.

The bones we keep
for broth.

If there is tomato to slice, it gets a little salt
and goes on the plate with the cheese.

QUOTIDIAN

If I have written out my lists—
poems, groceries, email replies—
and darkness still overwhelms me, I might do this:

empty the bathroom trash, unclench my teeth and fists,
go for a run till sweat pours. And dries. And pours and dries again.
If I have written out my lists

finished my coffee, eggs on toast, taken a moment to miss
all I've lost (I've moved or they've died)
and darkness still overwhelms me? I might do this

dance where I hit my pillow and pinch my wrists
and cover my head and ask, God why
if I have written out my lists

does the pain persist? The crying hurts. It is
an undulating headache. It is an audience while
darkness still overwhelms me. I might do this

differently. Sit in my pain as it hits
instead of running from it, hope it will die
or listen to it instead of writing new lists.
If darkness still overwhelms me, I might do this.

RERENGA

I *Kenehihi*

It began with dirt
plucked from stars
and formed into
a body that breathed

a little mishap
and then a curse
for the rest

a body hid whose
blood cried out
from the ground

II *Ekoro'ha*

the bitter herb of flight
from under a hand
too heavy to sleep
or grow under

look at the water
standing
like ears of corn
in a field

I was not alive to
see it, you did not
know me then

III Ioani

the word became
an empty cup
poured out

oil on a dry land
until a tender shoot
sprang up

was hewn down
and walked out
of the hot dark

a man with a ring
of keys around the wrist
a bit of fire in the eyes

I dreamt of
you whispering
the story

blood still dry
on the mouth

IV Waiata

All seven songs
sung from this ocean
rippled the horizon

a prayer is also
a summons

what strange ship
is this carrying me
through death
into life

onto this rocky shore
where the water still
sings to the wind

SEHNSUCHT

Cold Reuben, no cigarettes—
I expected something, but who can
know how they'll long to get back
to a place they've never been?

Do you know what I mean,
at times touching my side
and wondering at how I am?

The dark ocean from the window is still,
the waves are sparkling as in photographs
and all I can think is how I want
to cut through the sun setting on the purple horizon
with a pair of big scissors.

TUESDAY

Did you feel anything
in Plimmerton?

No, me neither.

RHETORICAL

Dear God, here is a ten-second pause

I'm back and I was counting the whole time.
The hills are wrinkled green blankets draped
over giant furniture. I want to have the sunset
mean to me what it meant to Emily Dickinson.
I want to talk to the supercilious sun about its
blue grey smoke lit up with the ridiculous pinks
of a dancehall girl. I want to be the dancehall girl again
twirling and smacking my bubble-gum lips, holding
onto the man with oilfield boots and wolf howl
in his laugh. Maybe I gave away all of my
books because they were too quiet. Maybe
I want them back because of the hole they can fill
in my bookshelf.

WHEN I HALVE THEM

the purple veins blooming in yellow flesh
remind me that home is far

WATER SONG

I watch the ocean, sky and seam,
fast red nights and long blue days.
I knew so little when I married him.

Does he take full-fat milk, almond or trim?
When it's easy to leave, why should we stay?
I watch the ocean and sky, and can't see

why one marriage sinks when another can swim.
Would anyone have known
I knew so little? When I married him

even the sun was young. One day, it will dim
while we are sitting on the rocks, old and grey
watching the ocean, sky and seam,

almost ready for that final sleep, lulled by hymns
the water sings. Sometimes nothing is the best thing to say,
but I knew so little when I married him.

We are taking our time, learning to swim.
Today leaving was easy, but we decided to stay
and watch the ocean, sky and seam.
I knew so little when I married him.

IMPASSE

The house is quiet and then the sound of bees
gather at my head. Will you let me be swallowed
by this? Another wave, another scalloped
rim of water on top of quiet water.

I'm sorry. I'm not sorry. I'm hungry.
Do you want me to go hungry? I'm not
hungry. Last night we ate curry and rice,
rice, rice. How can I come back from the dead?

A little tea. Have a cup of tea. I'm warm until
it's gone and then I'm cold again. Merino wool.
God, you made change for pockets and pocket
holes for girls like me. I'm looking for something
shiny on the tracks. I'm listening for the train.

INTERNATIONAL ORIENTATION

Homesickness is normal among adults even
three months after moving to a new country
especially if you have had any other major changes
in your life around the same time, or if you left
suddenly, or without farewell to friends or family.
Finances, food and weather are also
variables that may determine how long you
should expect to feel disoriented, lonely or
afraid of things that do not normally frighten you.

If the chances of returning to your home country
are uncertain, you may expect feelings
of doubt, anxiety or apathy to accompany
the usual sadness, discomfort and hesitation.
These are natural side effects and will subside
given you can create a stable routine and have
healthy coping mechanisms in place (see handout).

It is important to integrate into the culture you are
transplanting into. Many feelings of isolation and
confusion come from a lack of healthy interactions
with local people and customs. Smile often. Maintain
ties to your own culture, heritage and traditions
while creating new relationships and participating
in new customs. Your past may play a role in helping
you to understand why you feel the way you do, and time
will help alleviate some of these symptoms. If condition
worsens after six months, please contact Student Services.

MAUNDY

God, I believe in the big fish
that swallowed the man
and spit him back out.

I believe you were a man
with a hammer in your hands
every summer until you were thirty.

I know when you showed up late
to the party, water from the well
became the best wine of the night.

God, what do you think about
rent this month? Will you send
me fishing at Paremata for gold coins?

God, I believe in the woman
who hemorrhaged blood for twelve years
and was healed as soon as she touched you.

I believe you were the man
who slept through a great storm at sea
and cooked fish over fire for breakfast.

I know the rich man left sad when you told
him to sell everything, and when the desperate
came hungry, you fed them.

God, what do you think about me getting a coffee
from Vic Books with my last Edmund Hillary?
Who is it you hoped I would be?

PLIMMERTON

Here are the seagulls
and there is the shore.

Here are the fish and chips
and there is the store

that sells L&P for three dollars
ice cream for four.

Here's the red train station
there are the hills

like humpbacked whales
mottled with sheep

and barnacle houses
all facing the sea.

EXPATRIATE

it is like heaven
here and every
where else too
but some sad
-ness hangs in
the air and I do
not know if I
carried it or if
it carries me

LEARNING TO SWIM

When _____ happened it made me feel _____.
This is the first rule. It's like swimming, our new game—
the facts are false, the world inside is real.

Am I still in Vienna, floating from Klimt's *Kiss* to Schiele?
No. We are at our dining room table, I am learning how not to blame.
When _____ happened it made me feel _____.

I don't like this game, it's hard to breathe. Do you think we'll
drown? The monsters in my dark have not been tamed.
The facts are false. The world inside is real.

We are slow dancing in the grass, orange peels
scattered like rose petals, Edith Piaf singing '*Je t'aime*'.
When _____ happened, it made me feel

like a sliver of glass found its way into my heel.
I hide to keep him from the ugly growl of something maimed.
The facts are false. The world inside is a real

black mouth that swallows without teeth. An eel
that lights up the water and vanishes at the start of the game.
When _____ happens, it makes me afraid to feel.
What if the facts are false and this world inside is real?

WHERE STARS GO

After Dylan Thomas

Night falls in curves and lines;
if the sea moves, the moon gathers it to heart
and ripples the waveless sky. Send all of the ghosts
back to their beds, the calm of night
spreads its wings where no bird makes its home.

Little sun in the sky shines on the young
in their restless rage; where no questions stir,
constellations fall into the glass, are swallowed.
The bar becomes a stranger's bed, a nightmare sty
to prod electric girls with television eyes;

the whole thing makes a quick affair.
The old man's gaze is blank when he sighs a grey sigh.
The slow arrival of spring pushes through mud
and dies again each fall. See how the moon peels
back the sky to watch the pea sleeping in its pod?
Even the ocean hears blood

when it cries out from the ground.
By late afternoon, the loaves are devoured,
fish eaten down to the bones. What miracle
unpins the sail for the wind to wear it as a robe?
When the ocean stops moving, lift its lid
and ask what knots would be undone

by love. Night spreads its wings in rain
and ghosts tell stories of a man
catching hold of the biggest fish before it dies.

X

Electric beauty touches the lake
lighting up the trout in her sleep
(whose dappled body
escaped hook and net). Leeks
pulled from the earth under
full moon glow, dirt still clinging
to their white, webbed roots. Crystals
in caves shot through with light—
pebbles trembling as the train
roars past. The pied black bird
with a radio in its throat, singing
its terrible song.

KAPITI PROVERB

Angry clouds stack
on top of Liquorland from the other side
of these flat Porirua windows, and I think

why leave the whare pukapuka for
rain? On Sunday, a stranger
put his palm to my forehead and all

the rocks in my throat
disappeared. Had I even
been able to see before that?

It's getting dark.
Clouds travel south,
uncovering
patches of sky.

Is there a better word
than coincidence, for gold-
painted apples, framed in silver,
hanging above the exit sign?

When a word fits
into the air just right,
it's icing sugar on the tongue.

I step out into the street.
A night like this, clouds gone, the lights
are just pinpricks in a dark, dark tarp.

CANTICLE II

We used to picnic
along the highway—honey,
goat's cheese, a hunk of bread
or apple fritters from the farmstand
still hot and sticky in the cold new air
that is the beginning of everything dying.

LOG NO. 2

What do I mean when I say I am lonely? My second oldest brother
returned from Italy and is staying with Mom. We haven't spoken
since before I was married, but for no reason other than that he
doesn't answer the phone. It is not raining tonight in Plimmerton.
Someone else has a fire going, and my clothes smell like smoke
but I'm not warm. I'm not alone, neither is my husband, but if
you ask him how he feels, he will say, yeah me too, I've got my
own heartaches. He can write about that himself, it's hard enough
writing from inside my head. I keep remembering I'm in a country
that's different and familiar but not in any way I can explain, and
the sky is the reddest I've ever seen it. My dad lives in New Jersey
now. Not many people in New Zealand know that. He hurt his
shin a month ago after buying some new Asics running sneakers
because he didn't stretch properly or wasn't running on the right
surface and I didn't tell him I've started running too because I don't
know how much longer I'll last.

AUGUST

Where else is there to go once I've got
paper, a new pencil with a green eraser
and half a peanut butter and jam sandwich? If
I could erase one year of my life
what would fill in the hole? Or would I try
to blot off a day here and one there until I
reached three hundred and sixty-five, and fall
in love with the one who noticed my absence?

LAMENT

Walking down Wakefield
I see her at her table

through the lit window
on the third floor. What a picture;

hair wrapped in a pale pink towel,
cigarette in her perfect mouth, ghosting

the automatic movements of a woman
alone on a Thursday evening.

I didn't mean to look,
but there she was,

flipping through
Capital magazine.

When, I wonder, adjusting my groceries,
did I stop being her, and start being me?

BREAKFAST CLUB

Sometimes tired, a knot nests in the centre
of my back and I think a mother bird put it there—

the guardian of sleep built the nest
and preens until I lay me down and catch

up on rest at the end of those long days. I miss
four hours of sleep and I'm talking about guardian birds.

Try spaghetti on toast for the first time
at Windley School in Porirua. Smooth-faced children look up

from their colouring to see what I think. I like it,
and I ask Hemi to spell out his name so I can write

a tag for him, and let him choose from the book
which Spider-Man sticker he wants, while I cover a yawn

that is as far from disinterest as the east is from the west.
It's just early, and that bird opens her wings in my throat.

NGĀ RAUKORE

I walk on the sand
when the water is troubled
and the fish are blackened with fire.

I did not mean to be the bearer
of such a little revolution
but sometimes it's the only
thing that will help dinner settle.

Sat down yesterday right next to a woman
sneaking her chips on the train
blowing crumbs from her bag
into the air like a fairy, licking her
glistening fingers, not sharing nothing.

The emergency brake will not be
activated. No one will tell anyone
to stop crying. What does it look
like, worship shoulder to shoulder?

Tonight I collect
seashells from one part of the beach
and put them down in another, this
redistribution is just what the ocean needs.

Every night a sunset, and all of it
over-the-top romantic (in the end
of the eighteenth-century sense) with
spontaneous light and lack
of absolute certainty about what might
come next. Mother, I'm in Plimmerton

and if no one asks, tell them anyway.
Tell them New Zealand is what they
hoped. Maybe I'll go home
when the sea around the land starts
to bubble with a song I've never heard,
are you listening?

Steep little cliffs, the beatitudes
are beautiful, the poor trees without their leaves
are full of light passing by the train window.
The silhouette of this woman is magnificent
and next time I find myself beside such beauty,
I'll write a poem and name it after her.

PSALM III

When the roof is pried from
the house and I am a sardine
(blinkless before you)

what will you say to me?
I see your hills, and yes,
every night a different
sun leaves slamming the door,
rattling the handle behind it.

Do you see my collection
on the bookshelf? I have
a canvas duffle bag the size of half
a crumpet and it is full of American
quarters and dimes. Behind that
bag and slightly to the left
is a box of Beehive matches
and behind that is a postcard
of a red-bellied woodpecker.

When the box is closed, and the dirt
falls like rain, and my eyes wear silver coins
(while everyone else cries water)

will I be there in body, but with you
a ghost? I read your book
from time to time, my favorite
part is the ending.

LOG NO. 3

A cicada left her tree, she is in plain view on the deck. Her wings
(of course she's a she!) flick straight up and down—now still. Her
body is a black almond from here. The trees are singing a hissing
song. She's alone and not moving, maybe watching the sea, which
is gentle today, three shades of blue and one of green. There she
goes. Is she dragging herself? Maybe that is just how cicadas move.
I don't want to look away. Dad is coming to visit in a few weeks.
He said it would take at least a year to settle in and he is not always
right but a lot of the sadness floating around my neck keeps me
from seeing or maybe it's just morning haze. Maybe it will burn off
when those red flowered trees that I still can't pronounce bloom
or maybe my eyes will adjust or I'll get them checked at Specsavers
because my AA card came with a coupon for one free exam.

CRUX

My grief is hurried, muffled,
finally shushed like a child in church.

I will get no chocolate for a month
if I carry on. Years of this—

look at my collection of stars
(salt crystals shining in the windowless dark).

Who taught me to say fine when I meant
terrible. Awful. The whole world should stop.

At the market, a crate of oranges
reminds me of you: ridiculous.

The half-finished crossword puzzle
at the doctor's office too:

7 down – German word for impossible longing,
4 across – manmade structure that holds water back.

LITERATURE

to sit at the table with grown-ups
who have died knowing all there is
to know and wake in the middle
of the night
afraid.

LOG NO. 4

I was given a pink paper-wrapped parcel on Tuesday
with flowers on it and I imagined inside it would be the make-up
set I wanted for Christmas when I was eleven but instead
got a book about looming which I was fine with until I realised
my cousin who was only nine was in fact given the princess
make-up set and so I asked Grandma if maybe Santa had
made a mistake and given the wrong present—and then Mom
yanked me by the arm into the boiler room where the cat food
and diet soda and rain jackets are stored to tell me I was being
rude and needed to apologise immediately which made me try
to explain to her why I thought there had been a mistake and
when she said that I was being fresh I burst into tears but not
because I felt bad about being fresh because I realised there
had been no mistake I was simply never going to get another
present I liked any more—now that I was eleven I had to learn
to loom things from books with pictures instead of click open
the sparkly pink eyeshadow case and become a princess and
next thing you know I would have to teach at school and give
away prizes instead of raising my own hand to get chocolate.

PSALM IV

Did you know me then, when
I raced on wine bottles to the stars
and purpled my teeth like a squid?

I climbed the metal stairs to every
sooty roof and howled like a jewel
at the clouds. Did you put the fire

inside me that sloshed heavy, lava-like
and rocked me to sleep in the rain? I woke
for food and I talked to you fast and loud until

the bar opened and I could sit high
on the stool, so far from that sticky floor.
I still hoped the world held something for me

then. Tonight marks a thousand dry nights and I want
to show you something. It's a little cave
hollowed out by my thirst, a place for you to live.

CANTICLE III

He's working nights—
blacked-out windows,
hallway full of steam.

My lower back
's the magnet
pulls him toward sleep.

After his eyes
close—quietly,
I shut the door
behind me—

everything
so bright
it hurts a little.

LAST PICNIC IN TAWA

my thumb is a spoon
inside the soft green belly
of avocado

PSALM CXXXIX: IN TRANSLATION

You have wandered through me,
and know me. You know when I rise
and when I sit down to write, you could
recite my thoughts before I think them.

Your stars compass my journeys and my sleep,
you know me like a hunter knows his forest.

I cannot hide a word under my tongue
from you. You surround me with a cloak
of knowing, your hand is the night
and the day. Your mind is too wonderful
for me, it is beyond my understanding.

Where could I go from your spirit?
How can I run from everywhere?

If I build a tower through the clouds into the gold
of heaven you will be there. If I fall asleep in the black
of hell, you will be there, resting cool beside me.

If I lift off from the cliffs with the gulls, and my body
rests at the bottom of the sea, your hand will reach
for mine, your hand will pull me toward yourself.

If I make the night my hiding place, I will find it as
the noonday sun to you. Darkness conceals
nothing from you, darkness and light remove
their clothing in your presence.

You formed me on the inside, you covered me
when I was water in my mother's womb.
What can I do but praise you? The one who
knit dreams into a void and made a synapse
pulse electric before I had a brain to wonder.
You, with a thousand suns in your hands.
My soul knew you before I had a mouth.

You reached into the lowest parts of the earth
and made me from secrets you found there.
You keep all my secrets, but none of me is ever
hidden from you. You designed my hips and my feet,
you knew what I would bloom into and said, it is good.

I want to wander through you and know you. If I could
find one of your thoughts, I would live inside it. You
hid them in stars for me to search out, and when
you ran out of stars, you put one in every grain of sand
scattered across the earth. When I dream, I count them.

When I am awake, I am with you.

CANTICLE IV

He pulls apart crates
and pallets with his hammer—
saves the nails in an old coffee tin.

Do you like it?

His hand fits my waist
thumb to spine, palm to curve—
I've never been this small before.

Our bed is young wood
marked with pink spray paint
stamped with shipping logos.

Night after night
we return to the warmth
of each other's skin.

Even after we fight
my body aches
to be held.

When my face is set like stone
the pulse in my throat
keeps me soft.

Other nights, my mind
wanders dark alleys
while I lay beside him

in this bed he made for us
and I wonder what happens
if I can't find my way back?

PREMONITION

You live here now
in a small town

where the bases of mountains dissolve
into sea. Imagine it, because you live here.

That is your grocery store,
this is the church

and you need to learn names
even if you won't be here forever.

Will you be here forever? The earthquake
will be unplanned. The ripping you feel in your chest?

It's called love. It won't suffocate you
but it hurts. The bread you eat is real.

The dusty mountains
are not *papier-mâché*.

The kai moana rotting on the shores, smell it—
all real. You live here. This is not Purgatory

but the roads do
close and open

close
and open

like the lollipop people get
their messages from God.

APOKÁLYPSIS

When I ask if you still love me
I expect to be read a bedtime story
where wolf cracks ankle bone
before swallowing woman.
Instead I am here, a mermaid
swimming slow toward a hazy light.
When I whisper to God
what the end is, I am listening for the kind
of horse that rears back in the dark.

HOME

My unhemmed blue skirt, īnanga
hot from the earth, and the sun

—I wanted the place to live in me
winding mud roads and the sagging roof

of a wharenui far away. The size of a child,
his stone sprouts out of the grassy hill.

And here is the awa where women bathed naked
and men strummed the bodies

of broken guitars. When I couldn't get to you
one way, I found another. Now

I look out of the window of our broken home
and wonder what branch there ever was to rest on.

ASSAY

Here the gravel slips,
the shearwater nests collapsed.
The sharp-toothed stoats smile
feeding on baby fantails.
The paua suffocated and
the air is awash with rot.
And for all of this

the rose opens pink on its vine,
the sea gathers her dead,
crushes them in her sorrow,
and returns in waves
so blue, the sky retreats at dusk.

MÄRCHEN

Hood up, breath heavy with each step
I run quickly over the carpet of pine needles,

wolf or a shadow following close behind me.
I touch the key in my pocket. To say I hope

the chimney will unfall or the foundation
will unsink is useless. I want a wardrobe, anchored,

a place to hang each one of my dresses—
ghosts in a windless dark world.

RŪMURI

The crescent moon shore froths
white where it touches. The mountains
behind it sneeze clouds of dust
from rocks sliding into valleys. World
news reports, 'Two fatalities', and then nothing, stacking
notes against the table. Aroha is perfume in the air, pressed

until grief and hope release oil. We are pressed
together in the one open café. Barista frothing
milk like a lullaby, clearing tables, stacking
unbroken dishes, asking 'Eftpos or cash today?' The mountains
through the window are changing, just a little. Would
it be okay if I come back here every morning until the dust

settles? Later, I pick strawberries while Molly purrs, dust
and cobwebs clinging to her back from pressing
her body through the crack in the foundation. Her world
is now full of birds. No one will stop her from going forth
into the night as a hunter. This sorrow is a mountain
newly risen on the landscape of broken terracotta pots, stacking

chairs around shattered glass. Restacking
is another way of praying for stillness, while rising dust
anoints the living. The mountains,
we know now, are living, pressed
against each other, speaking. The water's froth
is white, the sea exactly the colour of sea. A world

map fell from the wall but did not break. New World
is receiving shipments of milk in convoys, stacked
in the cooler with a markered note, '1 2L for

each family please.' The sun makes fairies of dust
shining through the window, floating above the fresh pressed
news stacked near the checkout beside a mound

of clearance lollies. 'Controversy over Puhipuhi Mountain
Mining Project' headlines. Time to return and gather the wood
spilled across the lawn. Time to marvel at home pressed
into the ground like a stamp by the same giant thumb that unstacked
firewood from the shed like a tin of sawdust
tipped. Time to pull out of the caution-taped driveway for the fourth

time today, and sit where water froths
at the base of the mountains as memories numerous as stardust
turn to perfume the moment they are crushed.

CEDAR

I am twenty-nine years old
not three years married,

looking out the window at white mountains
and the jade or topaz or granite sea.

I do not know what happens next.
In bed, your eyelashes are tiny black bones of a boat

docked on your cheek. How many times
would leaving be easy for you, for me?

This staying is being built so slowly, it's hard
to see if anything has changed at all.

RITUAL

April is the holy month when
Ramika squirms at the table, then stills,
his sprig of parsley
(such a tiny portrait of spring)

dipped solemnly into the tiny bowl of tears.
Most of the grey heads are bowed
when he drops it into Mya's grape juice
and loses himself in fits of giggles.

Baruch atah Adonai for the vine,
the fruit, the moments of not being alone,
the children playing forgetful, asking questions

I need answers to. I come
to the table without him, surprised
at symbols of bare hands bringing
food to open mouths—bitter, salty, sweet.

The house trembles, a few books fall from the shelf
and Vivienne swears before diving under her chair.
Everything is still again. Where is he?

The bread is flat, pierced, passed around
and eaten with charoset; apples,
cinnamon, walnuts and wine.

The glass must be emptied
and then filled again.
I stare at it, waiting for something
to happen.

EVERYTHING RUINED

I never wanted another man
but sometimes, the quiet ache
of impossible vows covers the window
of our love with gloom.

There is a dull thrill
in the nearness of bodies in a crowd
that threatens to break our thread,
sending us to our opposite poles:
you, alone in cold shadows—
me, enveloped in heat and light.

But when you come near—
dark-eyed and wild
to kiss my forehead—
a rush of wind blows through the house.

Marriage is not staying at all.
It is consummation by fire—
trees brought low till the roots are exposed
in a scorched plain. Everything ruined by flame
until finally, a new thing can grow.

Notes

Rapha (Hebrew): to heal, make healthful.

Canticle (Latin): song.

'Unmaking' (*for Félix González-Torres*): inspired by González-Torres' work *Untitled (Portrait of Ross in L.A.)*, 1991.

'*Paysage Moralisé*' (*after W. H. Auden*): sestina constrained by variations of end words used by Auden in his poem of the same title.

Mihimihi (Māori): speech of greeting, tribute—introductory speeches at the beginning of a gathering after the more formal pōwhiri. Often take place in the evening after karakia in the meeting house. The focus of mihimihi is on the living and peaceful interrelationships. See the Māori Dictionary online at http://maoridictionary.co.nz for this and all following definitions of Māori terms.

Ko Matthew John tōku hoa rangatira (Māori): Matthew John is my husband.

Rerenga (Māori): voyage, journey, sailing, flight, trip.

The following translations were found in Bronwyn Elsmore's *Like Them That Dream: The Māori and the Old Testament*. Auckland: Reed Books, 2000.
    V   *Kenehihi: Genesis*
    VI   *Ekoro'ha: Exodus*
    VII *Ioani: John*
    VIII *Waiata: song*

Sehnsucht (German): yearning; wistful longing.

'Where Stars Go' (*after Dylan Thomas*): initial constraint included mirroring end words of 'Light Breaks Where No Sun Shines'. Constraint lifted after third edit.

Ngā Raukore (Māori): taken from James K. Baxter's 'Confession to the Lord Christ' in *James K. Baxter Complete Prose, Volume 3*. Wellington: Victoria University Press, 2015, p. 563: 'But what about nga mokai, the orphans? What about nga raukore, the ones who are like trees that have had their leaves and branches stripped off by the heavy winds of the world?'

Apokálypsis (Greek): an uncovering, an unveiling, revelation.

Īnanga (Māori): whitebait, *Galaxias maculatus*—a small silvery-white native fish with a slender body; a whitish, pale grey-green or creamy-coloured variety of greenstone.

Märchen (German): fairy tale.

Rūmuri (Māori): aftershock.

'Ritual': inspired by Seder, observed on the first two nights of the eight-day Passover holiday, celebrated from the 15th through the 22nd of the Hebrew month, Nissan. The fifteen steps of Seder include retelling the story of Exodus, drinking four cups of wine, partaking of symbolic foods and specific questions asked by children. In 2017, following the 7.8 Kāikoura earthquake, the first Passover Seder was observed on 10 April. Passover is a festival of freedom.

Baruch atah Adonai (Hebrew): Blessed are you our Lord.

Charoset (Anglicisation of the Hebrew root word for clay): a sweet fruit and nut paste eaten at Passover, the colour of which symbolises the mortar used to make bricks when the Israelis were enslaved in Ancient Egypt.

Acknowledgements

Thanks and praise to God, endless source of mystery and beauty, the one in whom I live and move and have my being.

Some of these poems first appeared in *Ika*, *Kiwi Diary*, *Mimicry*, *Ora Nui*, *Perch*, *SWAMP* and *Turbine/Kapohau*. Many thanks to the editors of these publications.

Thank you to Sam Elworthy, for your persistence and patience in making this book a reality. Thanks to Katharina Bauer, Emma Neale and the beautiful team at Auckland University Press. Thanks to Deb Hartnett for believing this work into print. Thanks to Victoria University's International Institute of Modern Letters for the opportunity to undertake a PhD where many of these poems were written, and to the Faculty of Graduate Research for generous support through the Victoria Doctoral Scholarship. Thanks to Anna Jackson and Mark Williams for invaluable feedback along the way. Thanks to David Lehman who encouraged me to leave New York City to study poetry in New Zealand. Thank you to my Cutler, Wicks and Hartnett family, and to my friends, who mark my life with their stories and hope.